a

My sis
you know

Thank you for growing with me :)

Keep growing, always.

—Kier ♥

Shedding to Grow

"I write for young girls of color,
for girls who don't even exist yet,
so that there is something there for them
when they arrive."

-Ntozake Shange

Shedding to Grow

A coming of age story for myself

Poems by
Kiersten N. Brydie

inhale

For You,

this is for anyone who ever doubts their magic
for the times when we can't win the day
for the moments of comparison,
and breaking,
and molding yourself back together again
this is for the new skin that grew where comfort once lay
no more hiding in the shadows of yourself
you did it
you've done it

i'm learning that
Sometimes We Must Shed to Grow.

Contents

planted

Dissonance

there once lived a black girl,
skin of tar and milk and honey
mind as wild as the constellations
beauty as subtle as the sun
she grew up suburb cradled
in the green house of a handsome mocha man
tied for eternity, it seems,
to the strongest woman she'll never be
she spoke love as her first language
always thought the colonizer's voice sat awkwardly on her
tongue
found beauty in tree branches hanging a bit too low for
southern comfort
wondered why the clay here washed so RED
she had eyes that saw everyone bleeding and no wounds
must be terrifying to be that drastically beautiful
and have no sense of discovery
she never had enough heart to love this earth of hurt
people
she tried anyways
she gained new wounds from the fall
there is a particular type of dissonance that haunts black
girls
we are both the ghost and the ghostly
how is it that we straddle the moon and bleed like the
dust?

Black Burrow | Where I Am From

I am from the place of all places,
burrow of all burrows
it is warm where I have sprouted.
always.
even in the cold,
not far away there was always the crackle of dark wood
roasting in the fireplace
always the distant prayer of Luther in the background
always noise
I don't ever recall my home being silent.
there was way too much love to fill a room.

there were always two brown children smelling of outside,
of oak tree, and bruised knees and popsicles stolen from
neighborhood houses. dusty of sneakers pitter-pattering
down the pavement, and all the loose change we could
gather jiggling in the pockets of our play clothes. the ice
cream truck would ring the alarm and all hell broke loose.
this, of course, was in the days when children, was
"chirren" and we begging for outside air the way my
daddy longed to slap my mother's ass after long days of
working for white men.

we sang our favorite song at the start of each meal.
dancing black fingertips into palms, lacing our love with
bowed heads and me and my brother's eyes peeking at the
food waiting to be nourished. if I didn't know 3LW and
Backstreet Boys, I knew God was great and God was
good. I knew he always had been. I knew I always had hot
baths and cool sheets and wet kisses on two sides of my
face. I knew these things. like the ass whooping my
brother was soon to get. and how the tears tasted each time
I wanted to save him from his own 14- year old actions.

I knew the people always hugged tightly like there was
some unspoken love between dark skin and light hearts.
there was always the shuffling of momma's house shoes
and nightdress, floating down children-stained stairs we
had just cleaned. and our rooms were always clean. Beds
were always made. laughs were always heard. tears were
always wiped. and love, love was always there.

I grew up in the clanging of pots and family feud in the
background. the warm silence of Drop Everything and
Read on my father's lap. in scallop potatoes and baked
chicken I no longer eat. in the bellow of Whitney, and
Luther, and all of Boyz to Men

in the blackest of berries
in the sweetest of juice
and people who sing praise into each morning.

I am from the place of all places,
burrow of all burrows
it is warm where I have sprouted.
always.
even in the cold,
not far away there was always the crackle of dark wood
roasting in the fireplace
always the distant prayer of Luther in the background
always noise
I don't ever recall my home being silent
there was way too much love to fill a room

The only place I have ever felt alive

is in these words
between these pages and stanzas and sonnets,
I sing to myself
in every other sphere, I am lost
everyone rustles about and no one stops to speak of it
to breathe it in
life without purpose is nothing and I don't want it
it takes too long to bring myself out of these books
and no one is listening
I am home here
I am whole here
this is the place I lay my head

when I leave,
scatter my poems among the ones I loved
let my voice carry them to a memory that smells of me
I hold a poem for each of you in my heart
take it in

this is my legacy.
this is the good I bring into the world,
and it into me.

loose soil

The first time I learned I was a poet,

I was in the brown belly of seventh grade
I was sure to have five plaits across my head,
still undoing them and lying to my momma
talking 'about how recess had my hair all willy nilly
I was sitting in both my parents' laps,
a blessing I now realize all too well
I was reading page one of my
so fresh + so clean
composition notebook marked by my name

being dark hurts sometimes, I say.
I am not the shade they call beautiful,
or girly,
or pretty at the playground,
but I am me. Ain't that enough?

the first time I learned I was a poet,
my life had forced me to write itself
all of 12 years,
and wet cheeks,
and deep smiles
brought me here unknowing,
and ready to pour.

Things public school didn't teach me

how to love myself
how to pick myself up
how to wipe the tears
how to stop the blood
how to love someone else
how to love someone else while loving myself
which of the two is most important?
how to write the poems that matter
how to breathe after your first heartbreak
how to not break other hearts intentionally
how to grow new skin
how to look in the mirror and smile
how to smile
how I don't always have to
how to love my body
how to be woman and black
how to be black and woman
how to be black and woman and working class and queer
and cisgender
how to check my privilege
how to navigate spaces
how to hold people accountable
how to hold myself

What will I tell my daughter who is Black?

when I conceive, grow, and love a black baby into this
earth
and she is born 60 years old
and the doctor asks why her spine
is already growing into submission.
when the nurse asks,
why at her 3 months check up
her eyes are already bleeding the color of sorrow.
when she is sucking supple nipples,
and takes just enough to almost nourish her
being sure to swallow in consideration
of her great, great grandmother,
who never tasted the breasts of her own mother
because they were too busy being shoved into the mouths
of white babies,
and white men.
when she is never her age.
always 10 going on 15,
15 going on 30,
30 going on "too old to still be mad at the things that
happened"
but too black and woman to forget.
when her eyes and fists anger at the blow
and she comes home
tornado of mad woman whisking down Hambrick Lane.
Spiteful like 124
when she burst through the door
with 400 years of confusion on her back,
and she is heavy and angry and broken, and thin,
and angry, and almost not here before my eyes,
ripping through the rooms
and falling onto her knees and asking me,
how mamma? how did I learn this type of pain?
what will I tell her?

How do we forgive ourselves?

for the envy in your eyes
for the poems you threw away
for the people you didn't trust
for the people you did
for the ones you loved, but couldn't love
for the first time he called you broken
for the many times you stayed
for the absent talks
for the empty sex
for the poems you kept, but couldn't bear to read
for the men who called you beautiful
for the men who didn't and settled on 'bitch'
for the hate in your heart
for the anger in your body
for the jealousy in your tone
for never being able to read this poem to your parents
for the places you haven't traveled
for the ones you did, but never learned to appreciate
for the feeling of overcompensation
for the fabrication of your experience
for the claps you never heard
for the ones you did but made yourself,
for the years away from church
for whatever took you from there
for whatever brought you back
for the searching of love in cold places,
for the need to be searching for love at all
for whatever it is
that broke you in two
and bought you this journal

It's like the whole wide world depends on a black girl

and I can't even carry myself
can't lift my head high enough to see past the soil
and here the world go talking 'bout
I built this around myself
like I don't love the sun
like I don't love the glistening stars
like I don't love a beautiful night sky

This, I know, is true

I know God watches us all. I know the back seat of church
pews, and Easter Sunday dresses, and the white socks with
the frilly tool around the ankles. I know the sanctuary has
become our safe haven, I also know it has been our
demise.

I know the wars waged in God's name.
I know slavery genocide and the shunning of his people. I
know Mani's parents stand in the pulpit, while their
daughter stands alone with her girlfriend. I know she is not
welcome here.

I know the space between man and woman. the hours, in
the seconds, before telling your parents you may not bring
home a husband. I know the first man was supposed to be
my husband. I know you can shove 50 lives into 21 years.
I know I lived them all. I know I can't fix him and it
wasn't my fault, but I know I blamed myself anyways.

I know I have my father's face. we think he has his but
we're not sure. I know my life is better because of a man
who left him. I know the first man to leave me was my
grandfather. *cancer took him home,* they say. I know I
inked his last words into my left wrist and let them slowly
become the mantra of my life

I know how short life is. I know how to cherish it between
eyes and baths and bodies. and smoking weed on a
California rooftop. and scraping the plate clean of my
grandmother's sweet potato pie. I know she always makes
one just for me. I know love can be the hours before, flour
and egg up to her elbows, singing in the kitchen where she
makes her home.

I know my home was in the suburbs. I know I wanted to be blacker than that. I now know, black is not a project in Southwest Atlanta. I know we made our own Africa every time we grabbed hands around the kitchen table. or got high off some wine, weed or whiskey combination on our back porch...swaying to Luther, under the patio lights, surrounded by lightning bugs or fireflies or whatever we wanted to call them that day. I know the mason jars we kept them in. how at the end of the night we had to let them go. I know that's where my mother first taught me how to love freely. I know I've been trying to remember since.

I know since freshman year, I've become a new woman. I know this new woman hasn't had it easy but puts on like she has.

I know I love to read. I know I store my life in books and call it poetry. I know poetry can kill you. you can write yourself into insanity. but I know, my first poem was my first taste of freedom. I know I've been breathing ever since.

I know when I couldn't; I had these sistergirlfriends who held me down like an oak tree. I know they wiped my tears. I know they stopped the blood. I know they helped me heal. and I know healing can look like four black women with lips curled around blunts. it can sound like *text me when you get home.*

I know the time it takes to tend a wound. I know, someday they won't need tending to. just remembrance of what brought them here.

I know I want to live a beautiful life. to wake on the shores of my continent, kissing my lover across their forehead,

and dancing to the live music at the market just down the
road.
and cooking rice,
and plantain,
and avocado,
and rice,
and beans,
and stew,
and rice,
and fufu,
and injera.

I know, I'll spend my days teaching.
my mornings writing.
and my whole life loving.

this, I know is true.

To the past lovers,

to the fists
to the slave trade
to my woman parts and black skin
to the homophobia
to strange men in parking lots with big hands
to the bed I some days cannot escape from
to the voice barely escaping my mouth now
to myself
to everything that has tried to kill me.

I am enough
there.
I said it.
I wrote it so it must be true

I am still picking parts of myself from the concrete I have
grown into
my body has been morphed into a question mark
turning me into an apology

to this body and the overworked days, I can barely stand to
hold it up
to all the women I have feared
and all the woman I am becoming
to the gap
to the unknowing
to the doubt daily crystallizing my mind

I am alive
there.
I said it.
I wrote it so it must be true.

sisters as spine

The root of my inhale

a black woman brought me in
nursed me from supple nipples
bathed me in rosemary and spread me with shea butter
swaddled me in sewn quilts and kente cloth
she taught me how to love when there is not much love to
give
when the world has sucked dry your womanhood
she showed me how to love myself
even if it is only in the small things
like waking early to cook breakfast
saturday beauty salon girl talk
or licking the spoon clean after hours of Sunday dinner
meal prep
she taught me what it meant to be a woman
how to strut
and read
and make my voice matter
how to turn heads and keep them looking
listening
and gazing in adoration

so for all I know,
I am here.
breathing
writing
loving
living
for you, mom.

This one is for the black girls

for all the women in this room
for how we fill a room
how we make a home of wherever our bodies be
has a black girl's love not saved you today
is it not the reason you are here
is it not the reason you keep coming back or black
we are the warrior women
do we not feed this earth?
from the beginning of time, have we not been sucked dry
to leave you well

this is for the black girls
the loud ones who take up so much space
who's laughter hurls from the back of their throats heavy
like saxophone silk
we turn a bathroom into a salon or a talk show
or a million shoulders for you to fall on
black girls know how to hold each other
how to pick ourselves up and keep it pushing
how to take the lemons we are served and birth a five-
course meal

there are a million black girl grandmas preparing their
homes as we speak
placing bibles upon brown knees
ushering for the church and their families
how many communities would survive without us?

this is for every black girl there is
those who gain attention and those who seek it
those we don't think about
or forget to notice
this is for you

for how you are often imitated but always in 10th place
everybody wants a black girl,
but don't nobody *want* a black girl

this is for the skin draped around your body
you leave a trail of gold in your wake
you invented highlight before a Kardashian was a thing
have you seen a black girl in summer?
how the sun bends down to kiss her
how her hair be an extension of herself
and it is always on point
point to any black girl and try to prove me wrong,
I'll wait.

I said this is for the black girls
don't you think it's time we get our praise?
everyone who isn't a black girl stand up,
clap for us

this is for the women who raised you
who broke their bodies in two for you to be here
your saving grace
your girlfriend
the sista who sits next to you and takes the real good notes
the teachers, custodian, cooks, and scientists
the sex workers, basketball coach, barber, and pastor.
this is for all of you
for all of us
we are what freedom looks like
we are how joy smells
we have dedicated much of our lives to your survival
to your undoing and becoming and undoing again
now, it's our time
NOW IT IS OUR TIME
we take the throne, we so rightfully held
so will the real Black Queens, please stand up.

Black girls sure do know how to hold each other.

I'm talking about that good hold, like real deep in the soul and you know ain't nobody going to have your back like your favorite bitch or your homie down the block. don't nobody love me like my kin. ain't no heart that full. like I always knew I'd find a shoulder there through every dark hole and failed love. and my sis would dry my eyes and administer prayers into my soul, hand delivering enough laughs to forget the pain. and she did say *I told you so*, but it was way low under her breath as if to say, 'baby girl, I have been where you been. done sunk that deep, and don't no –no good nigga- deserve a queen like you."

I remember this one time, I had this sis who drove an hour and 10 minutes in a thunderstorm just to dry my eyes. I'm talking 'about one of them Hotlanta hurricanes in the pit of summer, and to be completely honest…her windshield wipers were faulty. we been told her that, but *I'm fine* didn't sell with her. you tell a Black woman her sister is hurting and her own flesh falls to the ground.

We are revolutionary

...and we are revolutionary
we in our brown skin and wooly hair
we who love not half-time
we who love not half ass
we who love, because love was the only thing that kept us
alive
back on the slave ships
back on the auction block
back in the streets of Missouri
we with our hands up
with our feet strong
we who cry in silence
we who cry not at all
we who walk with the souls of kingdoms
we with our own history
we whose history is not taught,
only birthed down through the blood of black moms
we with 20 moms
with entire villages all raising up brown things
all growing from infertile land
we who grow somehow anyways
we who live like boom boxes
like Cadillacs
like hydraulic rims rolling through streets that ain't ours
we who always got ours
always love kin
always calling some other brown thing
brother
or sister
we whose sisters form love
form impossible light
form infinitive bonds in the collide of shea-buttered skin
of them black girl hips
of that black girl love

we whose brothers don't die
we whose brothers don't live
we who make songs of dying
we who make mantra of hurting
of being hurt
we who make prayer of tears
of being torn down
we who rise again anyway
we who somehow rise again anyways
we who rise
we who are rising
somehow we are rising
and we,
we are revolutionary

Ain't I a woman?
after, Sojourner Truth

like don't we shatter this earth?
don't you see life pouring from my middle, and if it
doesn't, didn't you see me grow some other child with only
the love that I can give?
like, don't I plant seeds?
don't my back bend, and arch, and shake for this world?
ain't I the definition of beauty?
don't I turn heads and stir up chatter in bars and
courtrooms and chem labs of how magnificent we come?
don't I make sisters out of the candy lady, and the softball
coach, and the sex worker, and the 5th-grade math teacher
and and and...
ain't your belly full of the last fruit I had to give?
ain't my own clothes clinging off your spine as we speak?
don't I speak?
don't my tongue conjure love with each bend?
don't I write the stories that grow the dreams?
don't I save the lives?
don't I save?
don't I?
ain't I a Woman?

Colored girls' song

ain't nothing like the tears a colored girl sheds.
ain't nothing like being three-fifths a man when you ain't
one, searching for your fraction to call home. your
borough to nestle into and be comforted by the
affirmations that you are at least *something*.

not one thing saltier than the rivers we flow. then the rivers
we drown in daily. then the very streams we fill to the
brim but ain't nobody searching for colored girls. we're
shh'd into midnight stories as a fable of black
superwoman. when we go missing, don't nobody lift a
finger. don't nobody call the police. they ain't listening no
ways, 'specially not for no brown girl body.

we ain't bodies. bodies ain't ours.
we enter rooms by invitation.
cook your meals. clean your home,
but where is a colored girls home?
where do we sing?
where we dance, and shout, and praise
where we human? where we home?
colored girls ain't got no home.
only too deep skin. only flesh far too resembling of blood
and night.

tonight we stand colored girls. we link like chains,
and we are woman as much as we are colored and we are
colored as much as we are woman.
don't you make us choose which fence we straddle on
today. we spent far too much time with our legs shoved
open. who built them through our backs in the first place?
our backs have been bent for years.
grandma ain't never stood straight.
we kneel to let you get a better seat.

how life look from up there?
colored girls ain't seen life head-on.
only pain and sorrow. only the soles of boots knocking our
faces in.
and we keep passing down this same colored girl blues. we
sing it without knowing.
how did I learn this song?
how the words morph into my skin like tattoos?
how they taste like home already?
how my mouth already taped shut?
I barely had the chance to use it, but I use it now.

we spit color into your ears. pray it rings like fight and
stings like fire.
colored girls know fire. we have been the first ones to feel
his burns. and we burn. we have been burnt.
had fire extinguishers blown through our souls.
we immune now. try again.
we the toughest things you'd ever wish to get rid of.
but here we are.
colored girls.
singing our colored girl blues. crying our colored girl tears.
knowing this life ain't meant to cradle souls like ours. flesh
like ours.

but we are here, anyhow.
we are colored, anyhow.
you've tried for centuries to blow us away. but we are
colored trees.
roots planted so deep and you can't see past the soil.

we are brown and black. and yellow and red.
and all the colors of all the rainbows.

and you just can't silence a colored girl's song.

Gratitude

I got love. I have infinite love for all the sistergirlfriends
who are the reason I'm standing here right now. my knees
are not this strong on my own.

when I die, God make me into another Black woman.
for I know, a suburban girl, with charcoal skin is waiting,
is praying,
for an angel who looks like her.

flowers and footsteps

Love that don't love back

from the time I was a little girl,
I have always loved love
I mean, what's not to love about it?
you open yourself up to the deepest parts of you
and, most times, someone decides to bathe in it
someone may even open up too,
and two people forge themselves together
I always thought I had that type of love,
looking back, I suppose it was me who opened
and you who shoved whatever you had left into me
but I never understood why I laid on my back for that type
of love
we always claim ourselves stronger than that,
but even if you came in darkness,
I lit for you
I want the reciprocity of love
I want to be wide open with someone who isn't afraid to
bear all of me
I've got a few scars left from the last heart I let bury itself
inside my wounds
and there are shattered pieces I can't fork out

but that ain't love, right?
even if you dress it with a smile?
even if you cave in on me?
even if I'm the one calling you back,
taking your own fragments and pressing them deeper into
my skin
that kind of longing is lonely
I don't care
I do care
I don't want to be this desperate for affection
I want it to come easy
and painless

and void of blood

but I always bleed don't I?
I always rip my skin from flesh
I ain't never seen you cry,
not like I do
your tears are still beautiful,
yet there is no beauty in love that don't love back
only whiskey and blunt smoke
only this poem,
on my couch
the morning after you let them stay

I have only ever known love from a distance

the backside of a novel
the front screen of a film
through metaphors and pretty pictures
and things I've never seen up close
but just once,
even if only for a brief moment in time
I want to know what all the poems are about
the ones that drip with full hearts
and clean knees
and dry eyes
I would taste it and never forget
I would carry that love with me
I would find ways to sprinkle a bit on everyone
gift lump sums to a magical lover,
and save a whole lot for me
if only I had the chance to feel

From a loving poet to a future stanza,

I am giving you ample warning
flee while you can
while the depth of your eyes
and the bridge of your nose
are not yet etched onto wrinkled paper.

while our first date is just that.
a first date,
and not a fantasy I have since decorated with all the
metaphors I can think of.

while you are still you
all of your private parts
and biggest fears
and wildest dreams
pretty and perfect
and human and whole
and not a poem

you are not a poem
a narrative I can return to when I have found news words

I have this bad habit of turning people into poetry
I want to remember you in all of your flesh and beauty
flee while you can

P.S. run fast.
It may be too late

Some assembly required

sometimes,
you build this entire life with people
you form traditions
friday nights in the city
saturday walks to the mountain
sunday brunch after church
you wake to the smell of scrambled eggs and buttered toast
you fall asleep in familiar flesh
and all the spaces in between,
you love with all you've got

and one morning,
just as quickly as this life was built,
it is snatched away
for there was no real foundation

you cannot build a life around a fairytale.

Vanishing | Right Before Your Eyes

how is it that everything can leave?
your toothbrush
your dog's left behind shed hair
the shirts I borrowed
all the happy love poems
the smile you grew across my face
our standing Friday night dates
the love from your texts
your texts from my phone
your name from my mouth
the memories we once swore to create
how is it that everything can leave
just as quickly as it came

Whatever you do,

don't grow into me
don't build a home in my arms
or write a melody on my lips
don't grow you roots any deeper into my flesh,
for when you leave
as they all have before,
I will miss you like my own skin

I guess seasons are changing,

and we just aren't equipped for the storm

And remember those months we lived in love?

not as smooth as I had hoped
but love isn't always satin
we were wool at times,
or polyester
but love, my God, nonetheless

Isn't it weird when you've never met your partner's ex

but you know all the things they couldn't do
you share all the spaces they couldn't fill
hold all the tears they let cascade
and the memories,
you weren't there to live them
but can swear you see them in your lover's eyes
they way they light up when you pass the park they
frequented
how open hands turn clenched fists at the warmth of the
stars they laid under
how hugs always seem to fit like hand-me-down clothing
it's so weird that you've never met your partner's ex
but you are more familiar with the things they did
then the lover lying in front of you

I loved you the way

a teacher loves a classroom
ink loves empty pages
streetlights love sun turned dusk
knees love prayer
prayer loves praise
and praise loves participation

the way
black aunties love porches
sunday afternoons love iced tea
cobbler loves the side of tinfoil
eggs love coffee
coffee loves sugar
and sugar loves your lips

I loved you,
the way two things were meant to love
naturally,
without question, concern or condolences

that was the problem, I guess.

The first time you see a photo of them together

it will break you.
that's all I have.
there is no poem that follows
it will break you.

I have been here before

I know how this works
the cushion of this love will wear down
we will feel reality breaking into our tailbones
longing will appear in all of the familiar places
in our good morning messages,
the hollows of our fingertips,
the bends of your arm
the spaces in our *I love you's* will grow distant
we will compensate with bodies
that will not be enough
we will try to save what was never meant to work
you will move on and eventually so will I
my poems will hold your scent for at least a year after
strangers in the street
lovers on this sheet
I will love you from a distance,
the only way I knew how

Promises

new love can bring back the same old scars in different
form
so beware of anyone promising to love you
with bandages already in their back pocket

they are going to hurt you,
believe this,
I promise.

The love after

still tastes like salt water currents
in fact,
it is even saltier than before
because you knew better

He was the kind of boy who collected knives

wandered around bookstores and coffee shops
searching for afros buried in novels
he found me there

this is for the next girl he cuts into
the gash won't seem like much at first
but before you know it,
you'll have looked in the mirror
and blamed yourself for all the blood

He was the kind of boy who'd charm body bags under your eyes

and compliment their beauty

He was the kind of boy you wrote entire novels about

spiral notebook after spiral notebook
he was the kind of boy you begged to read them to
he was the kind of boy who threw them all away

He was the kind of boy

who made *damaged* swim off his tongue like water,
made you swear there was beauty in being broken

He was the kind of boy you'll never forget

the kind you don't mention to future lovers
the elephant in the room
the kind no one talks about
even though everyone sees his aftermath
he was the kind of boy who morphed you into statistics
made you pray for better days to come
they did
he was the kind of boy who made you hate yourself
he was the kind of boy who made you love yourself

I saw you today,

and I came running
and you swept me off of my feet
and our arms collapsed around each other
bodies folding into familiar places

you brushed the hair from my forehead,
just the way I remember
and for that moment,
between busy traffic and classroom runs,
we were infinite
there were no recollections of pain
or tears
or daggered words

you whispered I love you
it was soft and faint and open

it took all of me not to fall into your quicksand again

I wonder why I'm still fond of drowning

I still search for me in your songs,

fingerprints
footsteps
remains of my body

I haven't found any.

I want to erase you from my poems,
but then there would be nothing left

Trying to make you love me

was finding a needle in a haystack,
three miles long and four continents wide
I had myself and a tiny microscope with a solid crack
down the middle
and two years down the line
I realized there was no needle
but I kept searching for you
knapsack of all my love in tow

Destruction sites

we are construction sites,
and at times,
I don't know if I am the bulldozer
or the masterpiece waiting to be built,
or just the rubble
all I know is we keep ramming ourselves into each other
and calling it love

Gravity

I held you down like gravity
but you were some dumb astronaut,
always believing in the power of some unworldly thing...
and never me
you were uprooted
and each time I stitched your branches back into the soil,
I was gravity
but whoever appreciates gravity?
you just expect it to be there as a punching bag for your
feet each day,
and I was.

Sometimes when it's really late at night,

or extremely early in the morning
the kind of hours that whisper through alarm clocks
and snore deep and loud and weighty,
I lay in bed writing to you
telling you stories and daily adventures
and I always end each poem with

I love you

I don't,
it's just muscle memory

In love,

I am the kind who takes one step forward and twelve leaps
back
always fleeting,
always running and calling it protection
always hiding from the sun, afraid of her rays
I'm told it takes so much to love someone like me
I know
I had been trying for 21 years
I'm just breaking the surface

Bruised fruit

I've learned that we are all bruised
fruit fallen or dropped or thrown
from trees and grocery bags
we all have our own scars
some are visible, woven into skin
others we barely recall obtaining
we all have dents and scratches
we all have things we are not proud to have experienced
we all have things of which we are ashamed
we are all bruised fruit
searching aimlessly
rolling around forest or kitchen floors
waiting to be scooped up
washed off
and tasted anyways

Love in the hair

we were lying in bed
mid-summer, high as a kite mornings
my fingertips found their way,
again,
to her hair
as if her kinks were home and I never wanted to leave
this time, I don't stop,
I just allow skin to roam through coils tied beautifully on
top of her head

she asked me if I ever wrote of our hair,
and I paused as if the question were a foreign language
I speak heartbreak as my native tongue, but hair?

I guess if you really think about it,
our hair is a lot like our hearts,
and our bodies,
and the two of us at this moment

unruly and winding to the beat of our own drum

You didn't know you could ride a bike

but you pedaled tricycles like BMX
didn't think you could swim,
but you waded oceans like kiddie pools
didn't realize you could whistle,
but you sang spirituals into each exhale

so when he says, you cannot live without him…
LAUGH
hard and heavy

you are the most beautiful bird.
wings, unclipped
ground, unknowing

you will breathe new air.
you will reach new heights.
and you will FLY.

Love is something you fall in

fall out
stumble over
make a home out of
live in for a summer vacation
return to only on some winter nights
it is moving
it is the ebb and flow
rise and fall
night and day
but mostly the day,
though night sometimes,
if you like that deep love
that meet me on Edgewood in your finest black boots love
that love we've all seen in the ruffled sheets of morning

love will come
and maybe leave
love will stay for as long as lovingly possible
you have loved my dear
and it hasn't all ended in merry days and happy nights
but you have loved,
be grateful for that

I think I love better because of pain

and I won't necessarily say better
but I will say stronger and harder
the love is more pure
and I find it in more places
because I know what it is like to not see love anywhere at
all
and to be asking where all the love in the world went
and to say to yourself
I thought this place was full of it
and it has vanished before my eyes

see I've been there
so I know love better because of the pain
we who love unconditional, have been broken
and I get up in the morning with intentional love in my
heart
and I fill this world with love,
my little segment of it
I pour it into people and places
I find it where it is not there and make it visible

and so I walk with love
I walk in love
we can call it naivety,
but I think loving after being broken is a revolutionary act

To my daughter,

there will come a day when the world will shove
heartbreak into your back pocket. I will always tell you not
to search there for companionship, but if your tiny hand
finds her way woven in denim and lost love...and if
somehow some man or woman has burst open your art
gallery and convinced you that you are not Mona Lisa
herself. remember this poem. remember dancing in the
rain. remember self-love EVERYdays. remember you
were born magic.

and I know that these words can't cure the kind of
heartbreak this world is ready to plague you with. there
will always be ice cream, and tequila shots, and my
shoulders for those kinds of tears. just know that before
you loved some silly girl or silly boy, you loved yourself.
and that is more than most ever do. and you will paint
masterpieces again. this time, they'll have more character.

This time,

the love sings, and even when it doesn't, it is a hoarse whisper as beautiful as the sun. the dark doesn't greet our home and you, you are still the most beautiful star. when I say *I love you* and mean it, you gather me into your arms and I am tempted to live an eternity in your warmth, I thought I wrote of love before…but it was a wishlist. it was our eyes meeting for the first time, it was my smile reaching its full potential. it was your fingertips. your tears, your touch. your love.

it was you.
it is you.
love.
and now I understand the fairytales.

seasons

2015.

the year of learning
the year I fell in love, three times
the year none of those loves stayed, not even my own
the year I learned to write myself in and out of heartbreak
The year four women taught me what love looks like in
shea-buttered shoulders and black girl tears
the year I loved a woman and kissed songs out of her
mouth
the year we sang together
the year I sang alone,
the year I didn't sing at all
the year of growth
the year I chopped all of my hair off because I didn't know
who was hidden behind all those curls
the year I told my parents
the year they loved me still
the year I had two works published in magazines
the year I lost too much weight
the year I traveled
the year I dreamed
the year I lived
the year of laughs
the year of pain
the year God forgave me for leaving
the year I came back
the year I vowed to stay
the year of undeniable, uncontrollable, unyielding and
unwavering strength,
I am so proud of you.

So here's to 2016.

the year my own skin broke me and I came back twice as hard and three times as strong. the softest parts of me found some other home and my bones grew a fortress brave enough to fight the depression. this time, I spent 365 days loving a woman and we shattered at the feet of each other. I'm finding, though we hold our own brooms, we are made of like material. the year my lips greeted weed far too many times and I rode each high into the sunset. the year of growth from heartbreak. this is my internal becoming. 22. a glorious demise of everything I once believed. a fountain of rebirth. I leave you learned and lost. another year of bravery. you gift me sisters, laughs, and legitimacy. I spent 5 of your months in search of freedom and here I am…somehow alive. somehow in love. somehow free.

2016 was a hard year for black folks

who knew that much pain could be shoved into a matter of
days, and we boiled at the seams when our kin did not rise
with us. death greeted our doorsteps. death climbed into
our beds. death forged its way into our homes, and death
took so much from me. snatched poems from our lips and
family from our palms.

and still,
and still,
and still, I can't remember the last time I met a black
person not full of magic. not becoming of something so
much bigger than themselves. I mean, even in that year. In
that mystical darkness, we found room to love ourselves
through meals, and the sour of liquor, and the Saturday
nights we threw our heads back into freedom because all
we wanted was to love and be loved by some other black
soul.

and ain't that black magic?
ain't that the most excellent thing?
how we churn greatness from our grief. and I know. I
know we didn't ask for the pain 2016 gifted us. but you
cannot tell me that you weren't saved by the soul of black
folks.

and somewhere, somewhere, somewhere, far in the
distance, a momma kneeled to pray. a daddy held his son.
big momma made a refuge of her home and we are here,
we are still here because of that.

I owe a life of gratitude to the sistergirlfriends who made
my back strong. to the brothers who spread my smiles. to
my ancestors. to the bond. to the backyard barbeque. to the
two-step at the family reunion. to my army of Black

professors. to the black man street nod. to the black girl,
'hey girl.' to the kickback. to the matchup. to each moment
of black unity.

to 2017,
I pray you gift us the type of black joy we've always
dreamed of. that we walk through your streets choking on
laughs. that your sunrise brings a lover to kiss our lips
whole. that you are brighter, because of pain.

that you heal us.
that you free us.
that each night, we come home smiling
and we come home,
and we come home.

and ain't that,
ain't all of that the most excellent thing.

Farwell 2017

I remember how much I prayed for your days in the year
before.
I swore all up and down that you would be THE year.
and you were the year.
funny how we are granted exactly what we wished
in your days, I found myself in darkness and made light of
me
all of the poems, I thought I had, disappeared,
and I had to carve the old ones out of my bones.
I wrote the stories I had only learned to hide from
and the lessons I learned…
oh the lessons
2017 was the year I became the strong I always knew I
could be
I live and love from a new perspective
I lost everything and gained it all back tenfold
my God.
oh year of darkness, you had mercy on me.
I will bundle all of your days into the memories I will
reach for in my back pocket
for whenever another year comes like this one…
I will remember.
what doesn't kill you, only makes you stronger.

Resolutions | 2018.

it's the beginning of 2018 and I really feel like this is your year. I know we said that about 2016 and 2017, but walking into this year even feels different. something changed inside of you this year. 2017 was a hard year. mainly because it was a transitional year, meant to teach you lessons...and lessons you did learn.

I think 2017 taught you the most about being and becoming your own woman. carry that into the New Year. carry this fire for Jesus, yourself, and your purpose. you are filled with so much purpose. your voice impacts so many people. there is nothing in this world that can't be yours. this whole wide world is yours.

do everything you have always wanted to do in this year. don't let fear, or anxiety, or waiting for the right time and the right people hold you back. do whatever the hell you want. drop people who don't understand.

every pretty face who walks into your life is not meant to stay.
know your value and demand it.

this year, don't beg people to see your light - friends, family, and lovers.
forget them if they don't.

be patient and dive into your family, craft, and this world. work on time management, your temper, mood swings, and solitude.

this year, write the book.
please.
it needs to be written.

see as many new cities as possible. network and become a
better friend. plan, but don't let that stop you from living.

although this is your year, you will be faced with
hardships. it is inevitable. learn how to heal from them.
learn from them and let them go. take your career to the
next level. find sisterhood. foster healthy relationships
with older black women.

be honest.
make money and make memories.

in Jesus name,
amen.

To 2018

this time, I don't have enough words for the way God has
blessed me
it's almost as if the whole sky opened up and shined for
my warmth
I loved the way nobody could have explained possible
and when I didn't,
those who loved me left a trail for my return
there were so many smiles in this year
so many laughs
so many opened mouth kisses
so much doggone joy to bear
I said my own name more than anyone around me
I sang my own songs
I wrote myself back into blooming

this is not to say there was no darkness
this is not to say I felt no pain
but for the first time,
in nearly three years,
I do not have room for tears to fill this page
you were here but you are not welcome.
this time, I acknowledge the grief and keep on pushing
this time, love is more potent
all I can smell is my sunflowers
all I can taste is my lemonade
I built the year I wanted,
brick by brick
stone by stone
before, I had messed around and forgot my magic
but you can never truly forget where you can from
I look back on 2018 and thank it for birthing me
I look down and it is my own two feet holding me up
wow, all I can say is thank God for the journey
thank God for the pain

and absolutely most of all,
thank God for growth

sprouting | new growth

I love myself.

it took me 19 years to say that,
and 21 years to mean it
but here I am

what a glorious way of becoming.

The blacker the berry

one day,
you will taste your own skin
and hum that song everyone sang to you
the one about dark berries and sweet juice
one day,
you will believe it

Yourself

you feel broken now,
but you will soon find someone
and they will decorate your tears as beautiful
paint the battle wounds that only you had the strength to
live through
they will smooth out the edges that have been roughed
over time and time again
somehow, you will find someone
who will never make you feel shattered again
I pray that someone is yourself

I've had heavier hurt take root here,

and still found wings to fly

I've had deeper wounds exposed here,
and still, have touched the sky.

Dear self,

it is okay to say, no
you don't need to explain
you don't need to justify

you do not need to break you back for others to stand

take care please,
self.

Shattered rainbows
after, Ntozake Shange

we are handed heavy things
sometimes it is a first love
or a hearty laugh
or a sleepless night
other times, it is a shattered rainbow

there will be days when your arms are not big or strong
enough to cradle all things at once

when this time comes,
drop one
shit.
drop them all

I am too familiar with everyone else's struggle and not
enough of my own warmth

this
is for colored girls with shattered rainbows
searching for beauty in her wreckage

brush aside the rubble,
sweep away the debris

behold.
you are still standing.

Captain

you are not this body
you are not all the things you didn't do
or couldn't be
you are not pain
you are not depression
you are an undying masterpiece
crafted
created
deep with intricacies that not everyone can water

you are so much more than this body
than these stereotypes
than this existence

you are not this body
you are not somebody's
you are all the things,
the experiences,
the life you have lived

ART

you are the painter
and if you don't like to paint,
become the sculptor

become whatever you want,
whoever you need

you are all you wish to be
you are Captain.

I've been finding poems in other places

in my eyelashes
and stretch marks
and whispered *I love you's* in the mirror
these are the type of discoveries that make me believe
that this is what freedom tastes like-
my morning mantras
my hour-long bubble baths
my name cocoon cradled in my mouth

this is the type of self-love that makes me believe
that I am poetry
walking,
breathing,
thriving
stanzas

Self-vow

I vow to cherish you
to comfort you when you feel all alone in this world
to turn caring for you into my number one priority
I vow to love you always
to push you when you're feeling stagnant
and bring you water at rest stops when you've had enough
to tell you,
you are beautiful
because you are beautiful
in the kind of ways that only I can see
I vow to see you
to hold you
to know you
I vow,
forever and always,
to be your self-love teacher
and to never ever allow you to stop learning

Love your blackness.

your skin, your melanin.
everything they mock and then try to artificially become.
love your hips, and kinky hair, and big nose,
and the extra meat on your bones,
and the way your family can turn a Sunday dinner into a
reunion,
the way living rooms become a sanctuary of trust,
and how easily music moves through your body and into
your soul,
your crazy uncles and crazier cousins.
love how women you barely know become aunts and
godmothers in a heartbeat,
how 'tender-headedness' is a real term,
how you are frequently imitated but never correctly.
love the black person street acknowledgment,
the all-day beauty salon visits,
and the gossip that brings us all a little closer together.
love your community.
love your family.
love yourself.
you are MAGIC.

And be black in it

some days,
the universe just seems to work in my favor.
the sun peaks in through my too old blinds,
and asks to shine for me,
and I let her.
my tea is just the right mix of strength and sugar,
pandora is playing all the good Lauryn Hill throwbacks,
and the joint rolls itself to a finish.
my mangos ripen,
just as the blender finishes its cycle,
and pour itself, all oouie and sweet,
into a mason jar I haven't seen in months.
the soap suds dance between crevices, and the brown sugar
I thought I lost
scrubs my melanin back the way God intended.
the shea butter is thick, so the coconut oil melts the
hardened mass
around my upper thighs
and my hips
and all over my black ass
and Toni Morrison reads Beloved to me
as I sit soaking in the sun of a mid-Saturday afternoon
and all the fine black folk are dancing,
and swaying,
and two-stepping to music we can't hear,
we only feel it vibrating up and through our souls.
this
is the day,
that the Lord has made.
let us rejoice and be Black in It.

For damn sure

I want to write to become a better writer
and love to become a better write
and somehow, in its dichotomy,
hurt to become a better writer
and write better because I have lived
and live better because I write
I want to see the ends of this earth
and turn the shores into poems
and smiles into stanzas
and smile better knowing that I can make beautiful what I
have seen ugly
and when I can't,
I won't try
I'll just write the ugliness as best as I remember
I want adventure for my poems
and poems for my adventure
and all the things of this earth journaled up in leather
notebooks
and ink-stained fingertips
and a mouth full of the lips of everyone I had the courage
to love
oh, to love
to write is to love out loud again
to make this life something worth living
and for damn sure,
something worth writing about

How we learned to heal

we cry through the pain.
we feel the pain and don't feel anything at all.
we say it is all worth it.
say the broken backs just build us stronger.
say strong is the only thing we become when we are done
becoming women.
we become women who forget what it's like to wake to a
new morning.
who live the same night over and over
bruises and bruises
broken and beaten
finished
famished
someone of us find freedom.
some of us don't.
some of us never own our bodies.
some of us do but gift them away in attempts to own our
bodies.
our bodies, be the only thing we share but never know.
and we prance around trying to find a home.
trying to find the world that curves around our soul and
makes us move
makes us feel
makes me feel anything better than this
feeling the pain is better than soaking in solitude.
I am the lucky one, I found this pen.
she found these words.
she built herself with them.
black girls birth a new generation hoping not to see
ourselves in them.
we write.
we grow.
we rebuild.
this is how we have learned to heal

You are worthy

of love,
of joy,
of Sunday afternoons bed stricken with happiness
of dandelions dancing through Southern manes
or brown fingers grazing your back with love
of the whisper of silence
of the beauty of truth
of the breath and blood of forgiveness
of shea-buttered lovers
of a lover
of a lover whose words bring wings to feet
of intact mirrors
of entire smiles across the bridge of your face
of dry eyes,
unless they are pouring at the magnitude of gratefulness
of the beauty of falling
of falling and finding your footing once again
of teaching and learning the right way
the kind that doesn't break you into silence
of YOUR own voice
of your OWN voice
of your own voice, you are worthy.

A love letter to my younger self
**Inspired by Solange's Letter to Her Teenage Self,
Vogue 2017**

hey kier,

I think that's what you're going by now. I remember in 7th
grade when you forced everyone to call you Kiersten-
Nicole because it sounded rich. or important. or boujee. or
just like something. you have always wanted to be
something to everyone. or everything to someone. your
heart, surprisingly, does grow bigger. you keep letting the
world in because that's the type of girl you are. you will be
bruised and tossed aside, but in time, you keep learning to
love.

you learned it first in your parents' eyes. you have always
been grateful for the freshman public speaking class that
brought them together, but it will take you time to realize
how much of a gift they are. remember elementary school,
when your mom was out of town and it was time for the
big school field trip, but you forgot your lunch. big bro
called dad and he rushed to the school with everything he
could find. a sandwich. cottage cheese. chips. an apple.
fruit snacks. and a Capri Sun. you knew, that day, that no
matter what time or distance separated you two, daddy
would travel the entire world to be by your side. the whole
school called him super dad. you did too.

middle school was a doozy. you heard after you grew up
that 'kids are cruel' but you never understood why. the
names you are called will travel with you. the boys. the
friend zone. the not-so-nice friends. that's where you
learned to wear the mask...how you became your biggest
critic. crazy how the patterns we form are shaped so early
on. your mother sees through all of this. one night she will

cradle you into her arms. she turns on the documentary 'dark girls' and she lets you cry, for hours it seems, into her chest. she is your gateway into the world of black girl magic. you may not understand until years down the road that her silence sometimes is the protest. that her sweet voice has seen far too much. but know, no woman will love like the woman who grew you in her womb. your mother is an angel.

throughout your years, you keep trying to define yourself. you are looking for a label that fits. instead of one that is YOURS:
1. the 'ballet dancer'- you truly loved this one, but you were so young. 16 and burnt out. the love left. but it will come back
2. the 'shave all of my hair off as soon as I get to college, outgoing, baldie'- lolol freshman year will be LIT, that is all I have to say
3. the 'militant activist' who doesn't wear bras
        turned 'poet' who encounters a lot of....leaves
            turned 'public speaker'
                turned 'blogger' turned 'Christian blogger'
turned 'natural hair blogger' turned 'relationship guru' turned...
GIRL. you and all these labels. still, at 24 you are searching for yours. how do you define yourself without them? the age-old question. maybe in a few years, I'll write a letter to my 20s and figure it out.

your early 20s will be the hardest years of your life. you didn't know what darkness was like and you will discover it all at once. depression was a word you use to toss around. and then depression was all you knew. the mask you wear will shield you from protection. so much so, that not even love will shine through. you've got to let love shine through. the books you read, the people you love, and the people you become cannot save you from yourself. I urge you to see a therapist sooner and do not grow angry with God when people tell you to pray.

lastly, to the 23rd. the year you literally fall in and out of love. this is a confusing year. life outside of college ain't what it's cracked up to be and your first "big girl job" ain't either. you will learn more this year than you have in ALL of the years before. you will grow into yourself in the most unimaginable, and beautiful way. family will grow a new definition and friends. my gosh, your friends... they will hold you down harder than you could have ever dreamed of. sisterhood is something you will have to seek out and form on your own.

but I have a spoiler. you will make it, baby girl. you can't even begin to understand how powerful you will become...the lives you will change, just by typing away at this little blog. if you could see you now, you would smile with 1 million teeth at how far you've come and how far you plan to go. I am so proud to be the future you. I am so proud to have witnessed the darkest of days turn into a thousand suns right before my eyes. just hold on a little while longer, my love. you will grow wings and you will fly. you have always been and will forever be, magnificent.

with every ounce of my love,
kier.

exhale

All of my love,

There aren't enough pages on this earth to thank each of you- for loving me, for growing me, for challenging me, for healing me. Each of you, every single one of my readers, keep pushing me towards growth. You all are the reason I have sprouted.

Thank you deeply, to my parents for always allowing me space to create, even when you did not understand. For encouraging me to be the girl with something to say and the woman with much to stand for. Thank you for the love. For the extended bedtime hours that you gave me, and that I gave to books. Most importantly, I want to say thank you for my 7th-grade composition notebook. That was *the* defining moment. That book gave me the foundation to shed.

Thank you, to every black woman who made this collection possible. I poured all of the stories of our ancestors, and aunties, and sisters, and friends into these pages. You are truly my spine. Thank you for breathing life into me when my lungs had no more to give. I would be remiss if I did not thank the contributors of *flowers and footsteps.* Here is your debut. Contrary to many of your beliefs, this book is not about you. It is about the ways in which love abruptly teaches us things about ourselves. Thank you for the lessons. Thank you for the once loves. Thank you for the breaking. Because of you, I built myself again with my own two hands. My God, what a blessing you have been.

I love you all for reading and for sharing in my continuous process of growth. May we all be courageous enough to look back on our stories, pick apart the rumble, and discover the masterpiece of ourselves.
With Love and Black Girl Magic, Kier :)

About the Author

Kiersten N. Brydie is a spoken word artist, creative writer, and avid spreader of #blackgirlmagic from Stone Mountain, Georgia. As a child, she was always fascinated by the world of literature. Growing up with the writings of Ellen Hopkins, Nicholas Sparks, and Stephenie Meyer, she found herself both intrigued and left hungry. In seventh grade, on a quest for words that felt familiar, she began writing poems in a small black composition notebook. Soon she would come to realize the gravity of each word she wrote.

Kiersten went on to receive a Bachelors of Science in Communication and Public Relations from Kennesaw State University in 2016. There, she was able to create and share space with other black women all searching for positive representations of themselves. During a Black Women Writers class, amid the words of Toni Morrison and Octavia Butler, her soul awakened. Finally, she thought, here are the stories I needed. Here are the words of my mother, and her mother, and all the black women who birthed me.

Kiersten is currently pursuing a Master of Arts in Mass Communication and a Graduate Certificate in Women, Gender and Sexuality Studies at Georgia State University. There, she focuses on media representations and narrative storytelling for, by, and to black women.

Over a decade following her first composition notebook, her quest continues with **_Shedding to Grow._** She coins this, "A coming of age story for myself."

keep shedding,
keep growing

I love you.

-self

27110977R00059

Made in the USA
Lexington, KY
03 January 2019